# LISTENING TO MOTIVATIONAL SPEECHES

## DISCOVERING THE POWER OF POSITIVE THINKING

DR. JAGADEESH PILLAI

Made with ♥ on the Notion Press Platform
www.notionpress.com

|| Dedicated to all wisdom seekers around the world ||

ꕥ

# Contents

# Contents

# Prayer

**"Om Bhadram Karnebhih Shrunuyaama
DevaahBhadram Pashyemaakshabhiryajatraah
SthirairangaistushtuvaamsastanoobhihVyashema
Devahitam YadaayuhSwasti Na Indro
VridhashravaahSwasti Nah Pooshaa
VishwavedaahSwasti Nastaarkshyo ArishtanemihSwasti
No Brihaspatir DadhaatuOm Shantih, Shantih, Shantih"**

The literal meaning of this mantra is: OM. O Gods! Let us hear auspicious words from our ears. O reverent Gods! Let us behold propitious visions from our eyes, let our organs and body be stable, healthy, and strong. Let us do that which is pleasing to the gods in the life span allotted to us. May Indra, inscribed in the scriptures, bring us fortune! May Pushan, the knower of the world, grant us prosperity! May Trakshya, who vanquishes enemies, bestow us with blessings! May Brihaspati bring us success!
OM Peace, Peace, Peace.

# About The Author

Dr. Jagadeesh Pillai is a renowned Guinness World Record holder, writer, and researcher hailing from Varanasi, also known as the abode of Lord Shiva. With a Ph.D. in Vedic Science and a range of creative ideas and achievements, he is a true polymath. He is the author of more than 100 books including Research Publications. Although his roots can be traced back to Kerala, the people of Varanasi hold him in high regard and affectionately consider him one of their own.

Dr. Pillai has achieved four Guinness World Records in the following subjects:

**"Script to Screen"** - In this record, Dr. Pillai produced and directed an animation film within the shortest time possible, breaking the previous record set by Canadians. He has also received numerous national and International awards and recognitions for this achievement.

**Longest Line of Postcards** - For this record, Dr. Pillai created a line of 16,300 postcards on the occasion of the 163$^{rd}$ anniversary of Indian Postal Day. The event also included a questionnaire about the Indian flag.

**Largest Poster Awareness Campaign** - Dr. Pillai designed an awareness campaign on the subject of "Beti Bachao - Beti Padhao" (Save the Girl Child - Educate the Girl Child) to achieve this record.

**Largest Envelope** - In tribute to the Indian Prime Minister's

"Make in India" initiative, Dr. Pillai created a 4000 square meter envelope using waste paper to achieve this record.

Attempted - **70000 Candles on a 210 kg Cake** - To celebrate the 70th Indian Independence Day, Dr. Pillai attempted to light 70,000 candles on a 210 kg cake, which was recorded in World Records India.

Attempted - **Documentary on Dhamek Stupa of Sarnath in 17 Languages** - Dr. Pillai attempted to create a documentary on the Dhamek Stupa of Sarnath, dubbing it in 17 different languages. The result of this attempt is currently awaiting confirmation from the Guinness World Records.

Dr. Pillai is skilled in teaching the Bhagavad Gita, a Hindu scripture, and is popular among young people. He has helped many young people improve their lives through his motivational teachings.

In addition to teaching, he has composed and sung numerous Sanskrit Bhajans and patriotic songs.

He has also written and directed several short films and documentaries for awareness campaigns, and has volunteered with the police in both UP and Kerala to spread awareness about various issues through videos and photography.

Incredibly, he has produced and directed over 100 documentaries about the city of Varanasi, all on his own.

He has also helped and guided more than 25 boys and girls to achieve world records through creative and innovative methods. He is a multifaceted person who uses his intellect and the blessings given to him by God to excel in various areas. He is both a teacher and a student, always learning and teaching, and is able to master any subject he comes across.

He is a selfless social activist and motivational speaker who has overcome struggles and failures to become a successful and enthusiastic individual with a rich life experience.

In addition to his work with the Bhagavad Gita, he is also an efficient Tarot card reader, Astro-Vastu consultant, and a talented singer and composer. He has sung the entire Ram Charita Manas and Bhagavad Gita in his own compositions, and has sung the phrase "Lokah Samastha Sukhino Bhavantu" in 50 different languages. He is currently working on a detailed and scientific study of Vedas, Upanishads, Puranas, and the Bhagavad Gita. He has also composed and sung the Hanuman Chalisa and Gayatri Mantra in 108 and 1008 different compositions, respectively.

Awards - Four Times Guinness World Records, Winner of Mahatma Gandhi Vishwa Shanti Puraskar, Mahatma Gandhi Global Peace Ambassador, Kashi Ratna Award, Dr. APJ Abdul Kalam Motivational Person of the Year 2017, Mother Teresa Award, Indira Gandhi Priyadarshini Award, Bharat Vikas Ratna Award, Udyog Ratna Award, Vigyan Prasar Award, Poorvanchal Ratn Samman.

# Preface

In this book, we explore the power of motivational speeches and how they can help individuals to improve their mental and physical well-being, achieve their goals and reach their full potential. We delve into the importance of positive thinking, and how it can help individuals to overcome obstacles, increase their resilience and lead a more fulfilling life.

Throughout the book, we provide strategies and techniques for actively listening to speeches, identifying and setting achievable goals, overcoming challenges, developing self-awareness, building self-confidence, practicing mindfulness, developing a positive attitude, finding motivation, and taking action towards success.

The book is designed for anyone who is looking to improve their personal and professional life and gain a deeper understanding of the power of positive thinking and motivation. It is written for those who want to make positive changes in their life and are looking for inspiration and guidance to help them achieve their goals.

We would like to express our gratitude to all those who have supported us throughout the writing of this book, and we hope that this book will be a valuable resource for anyone looking to improve their personal and professional life.

# I

# Understanding Motivational Speeches - What They are and Why They are Important

Motivational speeches are powerful tools that can inspire and empower individuals to achieve their goals and reach their full potential. These speeches are designed to tap into the emotional and psychological needs of listeners, providing them with the motivation and inspiration they need to make positive changes in their lives.

At their core, motivational speeches are designed to encourage individuals to take action towards their goals. They do this by tapping into emotions such as hope, excitement, and inspiration, and by providing listeners with the tools and strategies they need to overcome obstacles and achieve success.

One of the key elements of a motivational speech is the use of powerful, evocative language. A skilled motivational speaker will use words and phrases that resonate with listeners on a deep level, helping them to connect with the message and feel inspired to take action.

Another important aspect of motivational speeches is the use of storytelling. A good motivational speaker will use real-life examples and personal anecdotes to illustrate their points and make the message more relatable. This can be incredibly powerful, as it helps listeners to see that they are not alone in their struggles and that others have been able to overcome similar challenges.

Motivational speeches are also important because they can help individuals to develop a positive mindset. Positive thinking is a powerful tool that can help individuals to overcome obstacles, achieve their goals, and live a more fulfilling life. A motivational speech can help listeners to develop a more positive outlook on life, and to see the world in a more hopeful and optimistic way.

Motivational speeches are also important for organizations and businesses, as they can help to build a more positive and motivated workforce. A well-crafted motivational speech can help employees to feel more engaged and invested in their work, which can lead to increased productivity, better performance, and higher levels of job satisfaction.

Motivational speeches are powerful tools that can inspire and empower individuals to achieve their goals and reach their full potential. They are designed to tap into the emotional and psychological needs of listeners, providing them with the motivation and inspiration they need to make positive changes in their lives. Understanding the power of motivational speeches is essential for anyone looking to improve their life and reach their full potential.

*"The only way to do great work is to love what you do."*

*– Steve Jobs*

# II

# Learning to Listen - Strategies for Actively Listening to a Speech

Learning to listen actively is an important skill that can help individuals to get the most out of a motivational speech. Active listening involves more than just hearing the words being spoken; it involves actively engaging with the message and the speaker, and making an effort to understand and internalize the information being presented. Here are a few strategies for actively listening to a speech:

**Pay attention to the speaker's body language and tone of voice:** The way a speaker delivers their message can be just as important as the words they use. Paying attention to the speaker's body language and tone of voice can give you valuable insights into their message and help you to understand it more fully.

**Take notes:** Taking notes can help you to stay focused and engaged with the speech, and it can also provide you with a useful reference for later.

**Avoid distractions:** It's important to eliminate any distractions that may prevent you from fully engaging with the speech. This may include turning off your phone, closing unnecessary tabs on your computer, and finding a quiet place to listen.

**Ask questions:** If something is unclear or you want to know more about a specific point, don't be afraid to ask the speaker for clarification.

**Reflect on the message**: After the speech is over, take time to reflect on the message and think about how it applies to your life. Consider how you can apply the information to your own situation and how it can help you to achieve your goals.

**Repeat:** Repeat the key points and takeaways from the speech to solidify it in your mind.

By following these strategies and actively engaging with the speech, you can get the most out of it and be more likely to internalize and act on the message. Active listening is a skill that can be developed and practiced, and it can be incredibly powerful in helping individuals to achieve their goals and reach their full potential.

*"Shoot for the moon. Even if you miss, you'll land among the stars."*

*– Norman Vincent Peale*

ꟹ

# III

# Identifying Your Goals - Learning to Identify and Set Achievable Goals

Identifying and setting achievable goals is an important step in achieving success and reaching your full potential. Goals provide direction and purpose, and they give individuals something to work towards. Here are a few strategies for identifying and setting achievable goals:

**Start with a clear vision:** Begin by thinking about what you want to achieve and what your ultimate goal is. This will provide the foundation for your goals and give you something to work towards.

**Make your goals specific and measurable:** Specific and measurable goals are more likely to be achieved than general or vague ones. Instead of saying "I want to be healthier," try setting a goal like "I want to lose 15 pounds in the next three months."

**Set realistic and attainable goals:** While it is important to aim high, it is also important to set goals that are realistic and attainable. Be realistic about what you can achieve and what resources you have available to you.

**Create a timeline:** Setting a deadline for achieving your goal can help you to stay motivated and on track. It also allows you to measure your progress and make adjustments as needed.

**Break down your goals into smaller steps:** Break down your goal into smaller, manageable steps. This will make the goal seem less daunting and make it easier to achieve.

**Write down your goals:** Writing down your goals can help you to stay focused and committed. It also provides a tangible reminder of what you are working towards.|

**Review and adjust:** Regularly review your progress and adjust your goals as needed. If you find that a goal is not realistic or attainable, it may be necessary to adjust it.

By following these strategies and setting clear, specific, and achievable goals, you can increase your chances of success and achieve more in your life. Remember that setting and achieving goals is a process, and it may take some time and effort to reach your ultimate goal. But with focus, determination, and the right mindset, you can achieve anything you set your mind to.

*"Success consists of going from failure to failure without loss of enthusiasm."*

*– Winston Churchill*

ഇ

# IV

# Overcoming Challenges - Learning How to Overcome Obstacles

Overcoming challenges and obstacles is an important part of achieving success and reaching your goals. It is important to remember that challenges are a natural part of life and are opportunities for growth and learning. Here are a few strategies for overcoming obstacles:

**Identify the problem:** The first step in overcoming an obstacle is to identify what the problem is and what is causing it. Once you understand the problem, you can begin to develop a plan to address it.

**Develop a plan of action:** Once you have identified the problem, develop a plan of action to address it. This may include researching solutions, seeking advice from others, or taking specific steps to overcome the obstacle.

**Break it down:** Break the problem down into smaller, manageable pieces. This will make it easier to tackle and will also help you to see progress along the way.

**Be flexible and adaptable:** Be open to new solutions and be willing to adjust your plan as needed. Sometimes, the best solution may not be the one you originally envisioned.

**Stay positive:** Stay positive and maintain a can-do attitude. Believe in yourself and in your ability to overcome the obstacle.

**Learn from your challenges:** Learn from the challenges you face, and use the experience to improve and grow.

**Get support:** Surround yourself with supportive people who can help you to stay motivated and focused.

**Take action:** Take action towards your goal, even when it may be difficult. Remember that progress is made step by step, and every small action you take brings you closer to your goal.

By following these strategies, you can overcome obstacles and achieve your goals. Remember that challenges are an inevitable part of life and are opportunities for growth and learning. With the right mindset and approach, you can overcome any obstacle and achieve anything you set your mind to.

*"It always seems impossible, until it's done."*

*– Nelson Mandela*

# V

# Developing Self-Awareness - Strategies for Developing Self-Awareness

Self-awareness is the ability to understand and recognize one's own thoughts, feelings, and behaviors. It is an important aspect of personal growth and development, and it can help individuals to make positive changes in their lives. Here are a few strategies for developing self-awareness:

**Reflect on your thoughts, feelings, and behaviors:** Take time to reflect on your thoughts, feelings, and behaviors, and consider how they influence your actions and reactions.

**Practice mindfulness:** Mindfulness is the practice of being present and engaged in the current moment. It can help you to become more aware of your thoughts, feelings, and behaviors, and to understand how they influence your actions.

**Keep a journal:** Writing down your thoughts, feelings, and behaviors can help you to become more aware of them and to understand how they influence your actions.

**Seek feedback:** Seek feedback from others, such as friends, family, or a therapist. This can provide valuable insights into how others perceive you and can help you to become more aware of your own thoughts, feelings, and behaviors.

**Learn from mistakes:** Learn from your mistakes and understand how they can help you to grow and develop.

**Listen to your intuition:** Trust your intuition and pay attention to the inner voice that guides you. Your intuition can be a powerful tool in helping you to understand your thoughts, feelings, and behaviors.

**Practice self-compassion:** Being kind and compassionate towards oneself can help to improve self-awareness and reduce negative self-talk.

**Take time to be alone:** Take time to be alone and reflect on yourself. This can help you to gain a deeper understanding of yourself and to develop self-awareness.

By following these strategies and making a consistent effort to develop self-awareness, individuals can gain a deeper understanding of themselves, improve their relationships, and make positive changes in their lives. Remember that developing self-awareness is an ongoing process, and it requires time and commitment.

*"Success is not final, failure is not fatal: it is the courage to continue that counts."*

*– Winston Churchill*

ꙮ

# VI

# Building Self-Confidence - Learning how to Build Self-Confidence

Self-confidence is the belief in one's abilities, qualities, and judgments. It is an important aspect of personal development and can help individuals to achieve their goals and reach their full potential. Here are a few strategies for building self-confidence:

**Set small, achievable goals:** Setting small, achievable goals can help to build self-confidence by providing a sense of accomplishment and progress.

**Practice self-care:** Taking care of yourself physically and emotionally can help to improve self-esteem and boost self-confidence.

**Challenge negative thoughts:** Challenge negative thoughts and beliefs that may be holding you back. Replace them with positive, empowering thoughts.

**Surround yourself with positive people:** Surrounding yourself with positive, supportive people can help to improve self-esteem and boost self-confidence.

**Learn from mistakes:** Learn from your mistakes and understand that failure is a natural part of the learning process.

**Take risks:** Take risks and step out of your comfort zone. This can help to build self-confidence by showing yourself that you are capable of more than you think.

**Learn a new skill:** Learning a new skill can help to build self-confidence by providing a sense of accomplishment and progress.

**Speak positively to yourself:** Speak positively to yourself and focus on your strengths. This can help to improve self-esteem and boost self-confidence.

**Dress for success:** Dressing well and taking care of your appearance can help to improve self-esteem and boost self-confidence.

By following these strategies and making a consistent effort to build self-confidence, individuals can increase their self-esteem, reach their goals, and live a more fulfilling life. Remember that building self-confidence is an ongoing process and it requires time, effort and consistency.

*"If you can dream it, you can do it."*

*– Walt Disney*

# VII

# Understanding the Power of Positive Thinking - Exploring the Power of Positive Thinking

Positive thinking is the practice of focusing on the positive aspects of life, and it can have a powerful impact on an individual's mental and physical well-being. Positive thinking can help individuals to overcome obstacles, achieve their goals, and live a more fulfilling life. Here are a few ways in which positive thinking can be powerful:

**Improves mental well-being:** Positive thinking can help to improve mental well-being by reducing stress, anxiety and depression. When individuals focus on the positive, they tend to have a more optimistic outlook on life, which can help to improve overall well-being.

**Enhances physical health:** Positive thinking can also have a positive impact on physical health. Research has shown that individuals who engage in positive thinking tend to have lower blood pressure, stronger immune systems, and a reduced risk of chronic disease.

**Increases resilience:** Positive thinking can help individuals to be more resilient and better able to handle difficult situations. When individuals focus on the positive, they are more likely to see challenges as opportunities for growth rather than obstacles.

**Improves relationships:** Positive thinking can also have a positive impact on relationships. When individuals focus on the positive, they tend to be more understanding and forgiving, which can help to improve relationships.

**Increases productivity:** Positive thinking can increase productivity by helping individuals to stay motivated, focused and engaged. When individuals focus on the positive, they tend to be more productive and achieve more in their life.

**Enhances creativity:** Positive thinking can also enhance creativity by helping individuals to see new possibilities and opportunities. When individuals focus on the positive, they tend to be more open-minded and creative.

By understanding and utilizing the power of positive thinking, individuals can improve their mental and physical well-being, increase their resilience, improve their relationships and increase their productivity. Remember that positive thinking is a skill that can be developed and practiced, and it can be a powerful tool in helping individuals to achieve their goals and reach their full potential.

*"Life isn't about finding yourself. Life is about creating yourself."*

*– George Bernard Shaw*

ꕥ

# VIII

# Practicing Mindfulness - Understanding the Benefits of Mindfulness and How to Practice It

Mindfulness is the practice of being present and engaged in the current moment. It can help individuals to improve their mental and physical well-being and achieve a greater sense of inner peace and balance. Here are a few ways in which mindfulness can be beneficial and how to practice it:

**Reduces stress and anxiety:** Mindfulness can help to reduce stress and anxiety by allowing individuals to focus on the present moment and let go of worries about the past or future.

**Improves focus and concentration:** Mindfulness can also improve focus and concentration by helping individuals to stay present and engaged in the current moment.

**Enhances emotional well-being:** Mindfulness can help to enhance emotional well-being by allowing individuals to understand and accept their emotions without judgment.

**Improves physical health:** Mindfulness can have a positive impact on physical health by reducing inflammation, lower blood pressure and improve sleep.

**Improves relationships:** Mindfulness can also improve relationships by increasing empathy and understanding.

**Increases self-awareness:** Mindfulness can help individuals to become more self-aware, which can be beneficial in personal growth and development.

To practice mindfulness, one can try the following:

**Find a quiet place:** Find a quiet place to sit or lie down where you can be undisturbed.

**Focus on your breath:** Focus on your breath and pay attention to the sensation of the breath moving in and out of your body.

**Be mindful of your thoughts and emotions:** Notice your thoughts and emotions without judgment and let them pass without getting caught up in them.

**Bring your focus back to your breath:** If your mind wanders, gently bring your focus back to your breath.

**Repeat as often as you can:** The more you practice mindfulness, the easier it will become.

By practicing mindfulness, individuals can improve their mental and physical well-being, increase their focus and concentration and achieve a greater sense of inner peace and balance. Mindfulness is a skill that can be developed and practiced, and it can be a powerful tool in helping individuals to achieve their goals and reach their full potential.

*"Optimism is the faith that leads to achievement. Nothing can be done without hope and confidence."*

*– Helen Keller*

ꕤ

# IX

# Developing a Positive Attitude - Strategies for Creating a Positive Attitude

A positive attitude is the mindset of looking at the world in an optimistic and hopeful way. It can help individuals to achieve their goals and reach their full potential. Here are a few strategies for developing a positive attitude:

**Practice gratitude:** Practice being grateful for what you have and appreciate the good things in your life. This can help to shift your focus to the positive.

**Surround yourself with positive people:** Surround

yourself with people who have a positive attitude and who are supportive and encouraging.

**Learn from mistakes:** Learn from your mistakes and understand that failure is a natural part of the learning process.

**Focus on solutions:** Instead of dwelling on problems, focus on finding solutions. This can help you to stay positive and motivated.

**Practice positive affirmations:** Repeat positive affirmations to yourself throughout the day. This can help to shift your mindset to a more positive one.

**Avoid negative self-talk:** Be mindful of your thoughts and avoid negative self-talk. Replace negative thoughts with positive ones.

**Take action:** Take action towards your goals, even when it may be difficult. Remember that progress is made step by step, and every small action you take brings you closer to your goal.

**Have a sense of humor:** Developing a sense of humor can help to keep things in perspective, and it can also be a great way to see the positive in difficult situations.

By following these strategies and making a consistent effort to develop a positive attitude, individuals can improve their mental and physical well-being, reach their goals and live a more fulfilling life. Remember that creating a positive attitude is an ongoing process, and it requires time, effort and consistency.

ഌ

*"Once you replace negative thoughts with positive ones, you'll start having positive results."*

**– Willie Nelson**

ഇ

# X

# Finding Motivation - Learning How to Find and Sustain Motivation

Motivation is the driving force that propels individuals to take action and achieve their goals. It is an essential aspect of personal development and can be the key to success. Here are a few strategies for finding and sustaining motivation:

**Set clear and specific goals:** Set clear and specific goals that are meaningful and align with your values. This can help to provide direction and purpose.

**Break down goals into smaller steps:** Break down your goals into smaller, manageable steps. This can help to make the goal seem less daunting and make it easier to achieve.

**Create a plan of action:** Create a plan of action that outlines the specific steps you will take to achieve your goal.

**Stay organized:** Stay organized and make sure you have the necessary resources and tools to achieve your goal.

**Surround yourself with positive people:** Surround yourself with positive and supportive people who can help to keep you motivated and on track.

**Reward yourself:** Reward yourself for small accomplishments and progress along the way, it can help to keep you motivated.

**Stay positive:** Stay positive and maintain a can-do attitude. Believe in yourself and in your ability to achieve your goal.

**Stay motivated:** Stay motivated by reading inspiring stories, listening to motivational speeches, and keeping a journal of your progress.

**Learn from setbacks:** Learn from setbacks and understand that they are a natural part of the process.

By following these strategies and making a consistent effort to find and sustain motivation, individuals can achieve their goals and reach their full potential. Remember that motivation is an ongoing process, and it requires time and effort. It's important to find what works best for you and to stick with it to keep the motivation going.

*"Don't be afraid to give up the good to go for the great."*

*– John D. Rockefeller*

ꕥ

# XI

# Taking Action - Developing an Action Plan and Taking Steps Towards Success.

Taking action is the key to achieving success and reaching one's goals. It is an essential aspect of personal development and can be the difference between success and failure. Here are a few strategies for developing an action plan and taking steps towards success:

**Define your goals:** Clearly define your goals, and make sure they are specific, measurable and achievable.

**Create a plan of action:** Develop a plan of action that

outlines the specific steps you will take to achieve your goal.

**Prioritize your tasks**: Prioritize your tasks and focus on the most important ones first.

**Break down your goals into smaller steps:** Break down your goals into smaller, manageable steps. This can help to make the goal seem less daunting and make it easier to achieve.

**Stay organized:** Stay organized and make sure you have the necessary resources and tools to achieve your goal.

**Set a deadline:** Set a deadline for achieving your goal, it can help you to stay motivated and on track.

**Stay focused:** Stay focused on your goal and avoid distractions that can impede your progress.

**Measure your progress:** Measure your progress and adjust your plan as needed.

**Stay motivated:** Stay motivated by reading inspiring stories, listening to motivational speeches and keeping a journal of your progress.

**Take Action:** Take action towards your goal, even when it may be difficult. Remember that progress is made step by step, and every small action you take brings you closer to your goal.

By following these strategies and making a consistent effort to take action, individuals can achieve their goals and reach their full potential. Remember that taking action is an ongoing process, and it requires time, effort, and consistency. It's important to have a plan and stick to it, to be patient with the process, and to celebrate small wins along the way.

*"Successful people do what unsuccessful people are not willing to do. Don't wish it were easier, wish you were better."*

*– Jim Rohn*

ꙮ

# OTHER BOOKS OF THE AUTHOR

1. The Moments When I Met God
2. Kashiyile Theertha Pathangal
3. GURU GYAN VANI
4. Abhiprerak Gita
5. ASSI SE JAIN GHAT TAK
6. Hopelessness of Arjuna
7. The Soul and It's True Nature
8. Sense of Action (Karma)
9. Action through Wisdom
10. Action through Wisdom
11. THEORY AND PRACTICAL OF EVERY ACTION
12. LOGICAL UNDERSTANDING OF THE SUPREME
13. THE IMPERISHABLE SUPREME
14. Yatra Nishadraj se Hanuman Ghat Tak
15. Yatra Karnatak Ghat se Raja Ghat Tak
16. Yatra Pandey Ghat se Prayagraj Ghat Tak
17. Yatra Ranjendra Prasad Ghat se Dattatreya Ghat Tak
18. YaatraSindhiya Ghat se Gwaliar Ghat Tak
19. Yatra Mangala Gauri Ghat se Hanuman Gadhi Ghat Tak
20. Yatra Gaay Ghat Se Nishad Ghat Tak
21. MAA GANGA, GHATEN EVM UTSAV
22. Ganga Arti Dev Deepavali evam Any Utsav
23. Potentials of Digitalized India
24. VEDIC CONSCIOUSNESS
25. A Brief Introduction to Vedic Science
26. Kashi ke Barah Jyotirling
27. IMPACT OF MOTIVATION
28. Let's have a Milky Way Journey
29. Color Therapy in a Nutshell

30. Rigveda in a Nutshell
31. Yajurveda in a Nutshell
32. Samveda in a Nutshell
33. Atharva Veda in a Nutshell
34. Ayushman Bhava - Ayurveda
35. Srimad Bhagavad Gita and Upanishad Connection
36. Srimad Bhagavad Gita - an attempt to summarize each chapter.
37. Facts and Impact of Nakshatra
38. Astro Gems - NAVARATNA
39. Ekadashi - A Concise Overview
40. A Concise View of Hanuman Chalisa
41. Inspirational Gita
42. Nakshatraranyam
43. Summary of 18 Mahapuranas
44. Synopsis of 18 Upa Puranas
45. Rigvediya Upanishads
46. Shukla Yajurvediya Upanishads
47. Krishna Yajurvediya Upanishads
48. Samavediya Upanishads
49. Atharvavediya Upanishads
50. The Seven Great Sages
51. From Rocket Scientist to President Dr. APJ Abdul Kalam
52. The Visionary's Voice - Quotes of Dr. APJ Abdul Kalam
53. The Wisdom of Swami Vivekananda: Insights and Inspiration from a Legendary Spiritual Teacher
54. Ayurvedic Remedies from the Garden
55. Sages and Seers
56. Rising Strong – Motivational Stories of Women
57. Beyond Flames -Mystery stories of Funeral Ghat Manikarnika
58. The Origins of Tulsi: A Look at the Mythological Roots of the Plant"

59. The Holistic Cow: A Look at the Physical, Spiritual, and Cultural Importance of Cows in India
60. Arts of Healing
61. Exploring the Divine
62. Understanding Five Elements
63. The Etymology of Ram
64. Symbols of India
65. Voice of Change (About Speeches of Great Men)
66. She Speaks (About Speeches of Great Women)
67. Patriotism on Celluloid – Brief About Patriotic Films
68. The Music of Motivation: A Brief Guide to Inspirational Film Songs
69. **Unlocking the Secrets of the Dashopanishads**
70. A Cultural Mosaic
71. Ancient Traditions, Modern Minds
72. Ecos of Ancient Wisdom
73. Beneath the Surface
74. From Temples to Ashrams
75. Sages of the Subcontinent
76. The Art of Healling (Ayurveda, Yoga & Naturopathy)
77. Indian Kitchen
78. The Festivals of India
79. The Indian Epics Retold
80. The Power of Mantras
81. The Indian River Ganges
82. The Indian Architecture
83. Rites of Passage
84. The Indian Silk Road
85. The Indian Literature
86. The Indian Villages
87. The Indian Folks & Crafts
88. The Way of Buddha
89. The Ramayan of Tulsidas

90. Astrological Remedies
91. The Secret Power of Motivation
92. Secret of Developing your Inner Strength
93. The Secret Path to Motivation
94. The Art and Secret of Positive Thinking
95. The Secrets of Practicing Ethical Living
96. Indian Art and Painting
97. The Indian Herbalism
98. The Palette of India
99. Bharatanatyam to Kathak
100. Exploring India's Astrological Remedies
101. The Indian Festival of Flowers
102. Indian Handicrafts
103. The Splashes of Joy – India's Colour Festival
104. The Indian Science of Astrology
105. The Indian Mythology
106. Path to Enlightenment
107. The Indian Spirituality for Children
108. Aromas of India
109. The Secrets of Healthy Relationships
110. The Indian Street Food
111. Discovering America

# Contact

DR. JAGADEESH PILLAI

PhD in Vedic Science

Four Times Guinness World Record Holder

Winner of Mahatma Gandhi Vishwa Shanti Puraskar and Global Peace Ambassador

Gemology, Astro & Vastu Consultant - Spiritual Counselor

Consultant for designing World Record Ideas

Efficient Tarot Card Reader

9839093003

myrichindia@gmail.com

drjagadeeshpillai@facebook

drjagadeeshpillai@instagram

jagadeeshpillai@youtube

www. JAGADEESHPILLAI.com

|| LOKAHA SAMASTHAHA SUKHINO BHAVANTU ||

9 798889 519546

Printed by Libri Plureos GmbH in Hamburg,
Germany